MENTOR AND FRIEND

Who do we go to when we have questions about God?

How can we find help when we want to walk more confidently in the ways of faith?

This book takes a fresh look at the centuries-old tradition of having a spiritual companion to guide and to encourage, and links the wisdom of the past with practical suggestions for how to find such a friendship in today's world.

MENTOR & FRIEND

Timothy K. Jones

A LION PAPERBACK
Oxford · Batavia · Sydney

Copyright © 1991 Timothy K. Jones

Published by
Lion Publishing Corporation
1705 Hubbard Avenue, Batavia, Illinois 60510, USA
ISBN 0 7459 1911 1
Lion Publishing plc
Sandy Lane West, Oxford, England
ISBN 0 7459 1911 1
Albatross Books Pty Ltd
PO Box 320, Sutherland, NSW 2232, Australia
ISBN 0 7324 0450 9

First edition 1991

Library of Congress Cataloging in Publication Data
Jones, Timothy K., 1955–
Mentor & friend / Timothy K. Jones.—1st ed.
Includes bibliographical references.
ISBN 0-7459-1911-1
1. Spiritual direction. I. Title. II. Title: Mentor and friend.
BV5053.J65 1991
253.5'3—dc20   90-43024

British Library Cataloguing in Publication Data
(Applied for)

Bible quotations are from the Good News Bible, copyright 1966, 1971 and 1976
American Bible Society.

Printed and bound in the United States

To my wife Jill,
and sons Abram and Micah,
in thankfulness
for their constant encouragement.

Contents

Foreword

Some books are just acquaintances we pass within a hurried crowd. Some stay with us a while, becoming friends. And, here and there, some few are counselors that come to us matching our needs with answers. This brief, important book is counsel. Herein, Tim Jones reminds me that I am one of those modern pilgrims, grown up in a land seceded from God. To regain the lost territory, I will need a little help: A companion to walk with me, a guide to see me through the dim places of my spiritual journey. Really, all who quest Christ need such help. Without a spiritual director, none of us will take the quickest, straightest journey unto God.

A spiritual director is a friend committed both to Christ and to our need to know him better. Such a one can instruct us in the value of mentoring or keeping a journal. Such a friend might help us decide whether we should have a set time each day to pray or pick special serendipitous moments from what Jones calls "pools of prime time" for praying. But always such a friend is a friend to us and to our Lord: always such a friend is there for the both of us.

I found a simple glory in Tim Jones' work. He introduces mostly very old ideas—centuries old, in some cases—but his work, like a ring of keys, moved me toward my own soul's center, each key in turn unlocking doors I had closed upon myself. Like Teresa's *Interior Castle,* Jones' work crooks its finger to beckon us ever inward to acknowledge our deepest needs. But Jones' best quality is that he lives in the now. He is a guide who quotes liberally from ancient sources, but would not have us trade our current spiritual staleness for the mustiness of old libraries. Since nothing would be gained by such a barter, Jones calls for a freshness of the heart built on simple, more earnest everyday needs.

Tim Jones became credible to me by being himself what he encourages me to be. His words counseled and directed, ordering me to action. Like a parent, he put one hand on my shoulder and bade me shade my eyes in order to see the distant truths better.

"Love is not two people looking at each other, but two people looking in the same direction" (chapter six). This line expresses for me the heart of spiritual direction Tim Jones wants all of us to see. Spiritual directors are not psychoanalysts. We are neither Rogerian attenders, nor Freudian advisers. We who receive or give spiritual direction are there to clarify a view of Christ—that's all—and if looking together firms the vision, then spiritual direction has succeeded.

Spiritual directors are key people—but alas, they are only people. Therefore, we must never grow dependent upon them or expect them to be Messiahs who will deliver us from all our spiritual neuroses. This would not be fair to the director nor in the best interest of developing our own Christ-reliance. Changing directors is inevitably necessary for continued growth to occur, but to "drop" an old director as something of no further value cheapens both our view of the dignity of Christ and our appreciation of fellow believers to whom we owe so much.

Jones helped me to see that great spiritual directors are ones who understand that, as their disciples progress and mature, the teacher-learner relationship will evolve into one of fellow learners and searchers for Christ. For me, Jones' best phrase is "mutual mentoring." It is the proverbial "iron sharpening iron" principle (Proverbs 27:17) by which both director and directee become indistinguishable in their need. John of the Cross accentuates this truth when he calls all spiritual directors to remember that the Holy Spirit himself is the real director.

Jones' counseling in the matter of the inner life spoke to firm up my own weakness in prayer. "Pray" is the most frequent directive of this book. "Men ought always to pray," said Jesus (Luke 18:1). Jones understands this. We are to pray to find a director, pray to find out if we should be the answer to someone else's need for a director. We are to pray for counsel and then counsel in prayer. We are to pray for understanding and then pray in understanding. But prayer is more than godly chatter. Listening, not talking, is the essence. So, we are to pray and listen, listen and pray.

Jones writes with authority and yet calls with gentleness. As the pastor of a growing church, my present Christian world is usually over-glitzed and over-promoted. As a result, the private altar of my heart had become dusty, the ark of my private covenants was webbed over from disuse.

In this book, I am reminded it is my calling to walk with Christ in measurable growth. Tim Jones' book calls me to an uncongested and wholly reasonable altar. Since I want my devotion centered on Christ, I must let this spiritual centering take the nearest route to adoration. I need a friend who will keep my inner eye firmly fixed on the maturing majesty and the powerful simplicity hidden at the center of this book.

CALVIN MILLER
OMAHA, NEBRASKA

CULTIVATING THE POSSIBILITIES

When You Need a Friend

A soul which remains alone...is like a burning coal which is left by itself: It will grow colder rather than hotter.

John of the Cross

If one falls down, his friend can help him up. But pity the man who falls and has no one to help! ... Also, if two lie down together, they will keep warm. But how does one keep warm alone?

Ecclesiastes 4:9–10

A friend once invited me to join him for a hike in a bird and wildlife sanctuary on the gulf coast of Texas. After the hour-and-a-half drive from my Houston home, we parked the car and walked the gravel road that crisscrossed the flat marshland of the refuge. I saw only clear sky, clumps of reeds and a few waterfowl. It wasn't very impressive.

Merle, however, knows birds. "Look—up there!" he said, pointing to the sweeping wings of a great blue heron in flight or motioning toward soaring black-shouldered kites. Once he cocked his ear and had me listen for the rasping, eerie call of some grackles perched nearby. With the help of his sharp eyes and binoculars, I soon glimpsed a group of rosy spoonbills, with broad beaks and bony legs, preening in some marsh water in the distance. Merle identified and showed me every kind of goose and duck imaginable—more than I could name or now remember. With him along to point and explain, a new world opened to my senses.

This new awareness stayed with me. Jogging on the bike trails near my home a week later, I couldn't help noticing the colorings and calls of the birds near my house—most of which I would have missed earlier. My friend had changed my way of seeing and hearing.

Another friend helped me when I began to learn woodworking and furniture making several years ago. A true "do-it-yourself" hobbyist, I gathered book after book on selecting the right wood grain, using a lathe, making a rip cut with a power saw. But I best remember the expert advice of my friend Marshall. I spent hours with him in his wood shop. He would guide my hands in gluing and clamping a joint, and he kept my untrained grip from ruining the delicate wood I tried to cut with his band saw. He saved me from ripping boards and marring the finish of more than one tabletop or rocking chair. He helped in a way that my books, for all their advice, never could have managed. I gave up trying to figure it all out for myself, and I *learned*.

Experiences like these remind me that people cannot live well without friends' help. No one of us is wise enough to go far through life alone. "No man is an island, entire of himself," wrote the poet John Donne. "Every man is a piece of the continent, a part of the main." But because we often live and work with people who prize individual accomplishment, because we like doing things on our own, we may forget how much others can matter to our growth.

We need only pause and look around to see reminders. Take the centuries-old practice of apprenticing, for example, where a budding sculptor spends years under a master's tutelage. Or consider the modern corporate world, where a high-level executive will "mentor" a junior partner—critiquing the younger's decisions and introducing him or her to key business contacts. Or visualize the Olympic athlete's world, where the coach's expertise and disciplined regimen are as crucial to victory as the athlete's natural talent.

More than Chance Meetings

All of us have had helpers and guides, people whose influence lives on inside us in deep and sometimes hidden ways. Here or there a parent, aunt, school-teacher or friend has left an unmistakable imprint on who we are. We also may have found mentors in public figures or historical heroes—whose examples stir something dormant within us.

Even the author of a book that changes our thinking can be a mentor. A friend once told me of discovering

Alexandre Dumas' *The Count of Monte Cristo* as a youth. He was struggling with a dark, vengeful streak, and the book confronted him with his need to change. "I read it—and reread it in succeeding years—to remind myself of the futility of revenge," my friend told me. A decade later he read Gandhi's *My Experiment with Truth,* from which he learned that "trying to be holy was a worthwhile way to spend your life." An author can convey insights that effect enormous change.

Or help may come in the form of a letter or phone call. One man I know about took an unpopular stand against deceit and racial prejudice in his community. An old friend and colleague in another city heard about it and sent a note of encouragement. Years later, after the colleague had long forgotten the incident, the man appeared at his doorstep. He said simply, "I came to thank you. I had gotten to the place where I was about to give up. My wife and I were sitting, demoralized, in our living room when I heard the mail being delivered. I went to the mailbox, and there was your note. God wiped the windshield clean, and I started over again."

Guidance often comes in less dramatic—but no less important—ways. Such as in casual conversation over coffee with a neighbor. Or when we pluck up our courage and share with someone our fear of losing a job. Sometimes help comes serendipitously, without any effort.

We may want more than chance meetings, however, more than guidance on the run. Even if there is no crisis to be faced or emotional scar to be healed, we may want to benefit from a companion's help in a regular way—especially when it comes to our inner-most selves, the *spiritual* dimension of our lives. To whom do we go when we have questions about God, for instance? How do we find help when we want to walk more confidently in the ways of faith?

A friend of writer Tilden Edwards asked similar questions. " neighbor...confided to me that she had been going through a 'crisis of soul' for some time, but felt frustrated that there was no one she trusted to whom she could turn." She felt family members were not the ones to help, that Sunday worship did not deal directly with her personal situation, and that the priest at her church was too busy to see her. "So where," Edwards asked, "could she turn?"

Charles Swindoll relates a similar story. He one day bumped into an old Marine Corps buddy who had become a Christian several years after discharge from the Corps. But one thing was lacking, he told Swindoll: "I miss...that old fellowship all the guys in our outfit used to have down at the...tavern on base. Man, we'd sit around, laugh, tell stories, drink a few beers, and really let our hair down. It was great! I just haven't found anything to take the place of that great time we used to enjoy. I ain't got nobody to admit my faults to,...to have 'em put their arms around me and tell me I'm still okay."

I have known many people over the years who could say the same. They have friends, may even be active in a church, but still feel a vague longing for a friend who can help them grow in their relation-ships with God and others. One national study of contemporary people's spiritual needs concludes, not surprisingly, that every individual "needs a spiritual counselor or a faith partner of some sort—a person with whom to share his or her innermost spiritual feelings—a member of the clergy, a friend, a husband or wife, a parent, or a child."

The "Frail Instrumentality" of Another

Such a prescription is hardly new. The place of a companion or helper has long-standing precedent in religious tradition. The Old Testament, for example, is peopled with priests, prophets, and holy men and women who kept the followers of God from wandering too far from truth. In the New Testament, the twelve disciples' common term for Jesus, *Master*, suggests this constant need to be directed in soul matters. Many people, from a rich young ruler to an outcast Samaritan woman, sought Jesus precisely because he was a wise teacher and dependable guide. And Paul, the great New Testament apostle, called his coworker Timothy his "true child in the faith." We can guess how important mentoring and modeling was for Paul's younger colleague.

Throughout Christian history one finds many terms that name or identify this special relationship: spiritual director, spiritual friend (or companion), soul friend (an old Irish tradition), guide, and spiritual father or mother. Terms such as *pastor, shepherd* and *priest* also suggest our need for others' insights and guidance. Some call such helpers *spiritual mentors.*

Whatever our vocabulary, the growing current

interest in spiritual direction is based on a simple acknowledgment: To flourish, our relationship with God must be rooted in the soil of our daily relationships with others. There is no substitute for flesh-and-blood, kindred companions if we are to understand ourselves, grow in faith and compassion, and keep ourselves from losing our way.

"God has so ordained things," wrote Alan Jones, "that we grow in the Spirit only through the frail instrumentality of one another." The fourth-century church leader Basil told his readers to find someone "who may serve you as a very sure guide in the work of leading a holy life," one who "knows the straight road to God." And he warned that "to believe that one does not need counsel is great pride." Augustine, a leader in the early days of the church, likewise emphasized that "no one can walk without a guide."

All this confirms what most of us know intuitively: We travel best when we have someone beside us. A companion can help us explore the spiritual journey's sometimes bewildering terrain and steer us from wrong turns. A friend can keep us from drowsily missing the sights and signposts along the road of faith.

The Adventure of Spiritual Friendship

Over the years my search for such friendship has widened. It began in high school when Brandt, a crusty, bearded, countercultural Christian invited me to meet him in a restaurant once a week to talk about the Bible. Over pieces of pie, he helped me apply what I learned about faith to daily decisions. What did I want to do with my life? How often should I pray? How should I relate to my parents?

Since then there have been many times I have found helpers, especially at the turning points of life, such as marriage, graduation, job resignation or the birth of a child. The relationships have assumed many forms. Sometimes they have been informal, built on impromptu conversations in a parking lot or while riding in a car. Other times I have set up a formal, structured relationship with a spiritual director.

Perhaps most significant is my friendship with someone I will call Bill, with whom I meet once a week for an hour. We share with one another our stresses, anxieties, joys, even doubts. We give encouragement, prod the other to new ways of thinking, and usually pray aloud for one another. We help each other listen for what God is saying through our lives' daily routine. Neither of us is an "expert," just a companion and guide.

Letting someone walk alongside us, of course, is no panacea. But neither is it a vain exercise. The companionship we seek, and sometimes give to others, can open our eyes to things we would otherwise miss. One of the most wonderful gifts we receive from a spiritual mentor or friend, suggests Alan Jones, "is that of a new perspective. He or she is able to stir up our imagination so that we not only view the past differently, but also allow the future to be pregnant with new and exciting possibilities."

That could sound like a glib promise. But in the

chapters that follow, we will see how cultivating a relationship with a spiritual friend or mentor can help us find the way to a place far from where we stand now.

For Further Reflection

☛ Think back and recall times when the comment of a friend or teacher helped you understand something about yourself that you might otherwise have missed. How did the insight help you to arrive at a new perspective? Help you better understand your doubts or questions? Enable you to experience a trying situation and come through with renewed faith?

Does your experience match the claim of Alan Jones, who wrote, "Sometimes all it takes to bring about the miracle of new hope is a tiny shift of perspective, like a painter seeing a whole new landscape merely by changing the position of the easel"?

☛ Consider this comment by novelist Dan Wakefield in his autobiography: "There are in all our lives important mentors...whom we never meet in person but whose thoughts and ideas reach us in stories, books, essays, and poems." In what ways have you benefited from the wisdom of mentors through things you have read?

How has such mentoring been a legitimate—or inadequate—substitute for the immediacy of a flesh-and-blood friend or guide?

☛ What are the limitations of the "rugged individualism" rampant in our culture? In what areas of your life would you benefit from a spiritual helper and friend?

☛ Do some research among friends and family members. Ask them to tell you about some of the most influential people in their lives. If necessary, gently probe to find out how your friends' values can be traced to others' mentoring and modeling.

CHAPTER TWO

Great Expectations

A friend is the hope of the heart.

Ralph Waldo Emerson

*Great pleasure is given by a true friend who is
worthy of complete trust; who can give advice and
also take it; to whom one can lay open the heart
and confide all secrets, even one's faults—in a
word, a second self.*

Mademoiselle de Scudéry

A faithful friend is the medicine of life.

Ecclesiasticus, in the Apocrypha

*Iron sharpens iron,
And one man sharpens another.*

The Book of Proverbs

Tom was a freshman in college, living long hours from home, struggling through a Midwest winter of record-breaking cold. But he did make a special friend in Mike, an older and wiser classmate. The time they spent talking—in the hallways after class or in small-group meetings in the dormitory—strengthened Tom's faith. Mike became a true friend and guide.

But once Tom had to face an unexpected temptation—alone. When it was over, he was disappointed with himself and confused about the trustworthiness of his friend. He went to Mike's apartment and demanded, "Why didn't you tell me about this?"

"I was angry with him," Tom explained to me. "He hadn't prepared me for this hard lesson, hadn't alerted me. 'You're the wilderness guide around here,' I said. 'Why didn't you know the falls were coming up?' I had expected him to teach me everything about the Christian life and to be there for every experience," Tom said. "I needed healthier expectations."

If a mentor's help is no answer for our every uncertainty, what can we expect? What are the real benefits and limitations of such a relationship? Relationships of spiritual help should be based on a clear understanding of our hopes and needs.

The Wonders of Clarity

My friend Bill and I found it crucial to talk openly about what we expected from our weekly meetings. We were clear, for example, about the kind of commitment we were making. We began by honestly admitting that it might not work. This would be an experiment; we would meet for a specified time—four weeks—and then evaluate.

"I knew," Bill told me later, "that if our 'experiment' didn't work, if the relationship ended up not being mutually agreeable and helpful, we could quit—and still be friends. I knew that if for any reason one of us pulled out, I could still stop by your office or say hello if I bumped into you in the hallway."

We also made it clear that we saw this as a relationship of mutual mentoring; one would not look to the other as a parent or answer-giver. Neither of us was looking to the other for intensive psychological analysis or in-depth counseling; we were there simply to support and to help each other grow spiritually.

Rob and Gary took a similar approach. They spent time together jogging, playing racquetball and just talking. When each discovered that the other could be relied upon as a sounding board, they agreed to meet together once a week.

They established from the outset that neither would feel pressure to tell all. "We weren't each other's therapists," Gary said, "but rather friends who would help each other in the spiritual life. We wouldn't try to change the other person but would work together on changing ourselves."

There is another reason for having a clear understanding of mutual expectations. Sometimes the most helpful arrangement is not one of mutual mentoring, but of a wiser (perhaps older) guide helping a beginner. If so, it can happen, as it did with my friend Louise, that the beginner will develop feelings of friendship and admiration that are not reciprocated by the elder partner. Louise was devastated to learn after several months that her mentor did not include her in his circle of personal friends. He cared about her and wanted to help, but was not looking for the intimacy of friendship.

Clear expectations, then, will help us know what we can anticipate from another's help and companionship.

The Good We *Can* Expect

In addition to helping us avoid disillusionment, positive expectations can motivate us to cultivate spiritual friendship. Here are some reasonable hopes for a relationship with a helper or special friend:

Expect to find immense support simply from another's presence. More important than any advice someone may offer is the assurance of support. It is encouraging to know that we do not face the battles of daily life and spiritual growth alone.

Peter, a man in his thirties, appreciated this kind of companionship. "In the beginning, almost every week that I met with my friend I had to admit that I had given practically no time to prayer the week before. As that went on week after week, it became harder for me to see myself as a spiritual giant. I had to admit that for all my talk, sometimes I don't care about prayer or reading the Bible. But every week, I found that my friend would listen to me. I realized, 'He's going to like me even if I'm like this.' It was freeing to understand I could just be who I was."

Such a climate of support and freedom is indispensable to growth. Such a friend helps us not to grow weary and lose the hope that keeps us trying.

Expect a spiritual guide to help make new sense of everyday life. I sometimes think that my anxiety about paying next month's bills has little to do with my spiritual life. But my mentor resists the temptation to talk only of "spiritual" things. He realizes that from the moment my morning alarm jars me awake until the house grows quiet at night, God is at work in my life—in the dramatic *and* the ordinary.

Some time ago, while walking down the main street shopping district of a nearby town, I ran into an executive of the company I work for. I had talked with him several times at work, but seeing him suddenly in front of me left me flustered. We exchanged pleasantries, but I looked back with frustration on my awkwardness during the conversation.

Later I told the woman who was then my mentor of my self-consciousness in the encounter. "What did the experience tell you?" she asked. Then she added, "Anytime we rub our noses in our own humanity, there is a gift in it—even if it's a bit uncomfortable to experience. God tells us things about ourselves through what happens to us." We went on to talk about both my overactive concern with my image and my need to accept myself as I was. My unexpected downtown meeting became the occasion for spiritual insight and renewed self-understanding.

While I tend to look for God in crises and turning

points, a guide can help me find God in the mundane and unexciting. He does this not by freely giving advice—which anyone can do—but by helping me to see the significance of my life's events and by praying for my daily concerns.

"[It may be simply] taking your children to school and kissing your wife good-bye," writes novelist and minister Frederick Buechner. "Eating lunch with a friend. Trying to do a decent day's work... There is no event so commonplace but that God is present within it, always hiddenly, always leaving you room to recognize him or not recognize him, but all the more fascinatingly because of that, all the more compellingly and hauntingly." My friends have helped me to learn that—and to stay alert while I balance my checkbook.

Expect a guide to help ground the spiritual life in something more solid than private experience or personal opinion. How spiritual some of my private ambitions sometimes seem—and how cleverly correct my excuses for not doing good! Until, that is, a friend sees my mixed motives and has the courage to tell me. Or when my schedule crowds out time for exercise or prayer or family relationships, I need someone to remind me that the tasks that seem so urgent may not be worth the compromises. A friend can help me balance competing demands and bring my choices into harmony with Scripture.

A friend can also help me when I am tempted to give in to feelings of worthlessness. When powerful inner voices (or others' criticisms) condemn me, my friend reminds me that I am still cherished by God. He can build the courage in me that allows me to base my life on something more profound than others' approval.

"If sin is self-deceiving," writes James Houston, "then I need a soul friend to give me insights into the ways I am deceived, or insensitive, or hardened... I cannot do it alone. Self-examination can take me only so far. I need others to help expose and help me understand where sin would deceive and confuse me." The path of spiritual growth holds too many pitfalls and wrong turns for it to be a private enterprise. A proverb says that he who is his own doctor has a fool for a doctor. There are areas—whether caring for our bodies or caring for our souls—in which we cannot be completely objective.

When one man was asked, "To whom are you accountable?" he remembers proudly responding, "To no one but God!" The shallowness of that answer began to haunt him, and he soon realized that serious journeyers need direction for their growth. Soon he was searching for a spiritual guide.

Thomas à Kempis, author of the devotional classic *The Imitation of Christ*, wrote, "Always take counsel with a wise and conscientious man. Desire to be instructed and governed by others rather than to follow your own ingenuity." He knew how valuable a trusted guide can be.

Of course, those to whom we turn for help must be worthy of our confidence. A guide who in blindness or ignorance takes us down *wrong* paths is worse than no guide at all. So how do we discern the marks of maturity that make for a trustworthy guide? The next chapter will offer some pointers.

For Further Reflection

☛ List some of the ways in which you think a spiritual friend or guide could help you. What, for example, are some of your greatest needs in your relationship with God? Have you ever said to yourself (or another), "I wish I had someone to talk to about my spiritual struggles"?

☛ Consider these safeguards that will minimize misunderstandings as you begin a relationship with a spiritual companion:

Talk over and define expectations as you begin meeting with your partner. Discuss such things as frequency of meeting and what happens during your times together.

Be clear about whether spiritual direction will be just for you or mutual. Are you looking for help for yourself from an experienced guide, or are you looking for a peer relationship?

Establish a set number of meetings after which you can evaluate, terminate or renegotiate the relationship. This will avoid much awkwardness if needs change or the relationship does not work out, and it will provide an opportunity for refining the purposes of your meetings.

☞ Recall a relationship in your past where your expectations exceeded the reality. Ask yourself if your disappointment or hurt might keep you from being vulnerable and honest with others.

☞ Take a step that will allow you once again to risk deep sharing. Steps might include clearing the air by talking with the person who let you down; consciously forgiving someone, living or dead, who disappointed you; praying for the inner healing of your bitterness; or talking about your hurt feelings with a trusted friend.

The Unshakable Companion

Friendship is a sheltering tree.

Samuel Taylor Coleridge

Though, to my dull eyes seeing,
Truth's clear light
Shines faint, far off in heaven—star-like, by night...
Yet will I trust in this: To thine still
Both earth and heaven with Truth's own beams are
bright.

W.C. Davies, sonnet to friend George MacDonald

Test the physician before you open yourself to him.
Determine whether he can be ill with one who is
ill, weep with one who weeps. See whether he
imparts instruction with gentleness and
forbearance.

Origen, third-century Christian philosopher

Some directors perpetrate great insult and irreverence by putting their clumsy hand where God is working... They may mean well, but they err through insufficient knowledge. Still, this is no excuse for the advice they rashly give without first understanding the way the soul is taking.

John of the Cross

Not long after my wide-eyed walk with Merle through the Texas gulf-coast marshlands, an unexpected letter and package from another friend, Jim, came in the mail. What he sent opened my eyes even more.

I had just met Jim, a struggling author with a balding head, flourishing beard and warm eyes, at a conference where he had been a speaker. After the conference, in response to a conversation we had there, he mailed me three books. As he told me in his letter, each volume had helped him negotiate some anxious moments of financial difficulty.

The three writers told of learning to depend more fully on God for daily needs. The books, wrote Jim, "helped to convince me that it is possible to live by faith, to place even financial matters in God's hands." In the correspondence that followed, he told me about his own setbacks and successes as he experimented with a more carefree approach to his material needs. The books, and his experiences, made me more aware of God's ability to provide.

So much so that, when my wife and family and I

decided to move from a suburb in the southern part of the United States to a small town in the Midwest, we did not insist on settling in advance every detail related to our new jobs and future income. We were more willing to brave uncertainty. My friend's simplicity and faith were contagious.

Our most significant encounters with others tend to be unspectacular. It is tempting to look for help from the experts and the notables, to look to the famous or the fabulous, whose mere suggestions we think should revolutionize our inner worlds. But a mentor or friend more often will point us back to the raw material of our lives. A mentor will listen to us and encourage us, helping us hear what God is saying through the wisdom of spiritual truth and the events of our lives.

There are several traits or qualities, then, to look for in a spiritual guide. Here are some of the most important ones:

The Openness of a Listening Friend

Perhaps nothing fosters a climate of growth more dramatically than listening. Dietrich Bonhoeffer even wrote about the *ministry* of listening. "Many people [like you and me] are looking for an ear that will listen... They do not find it among [some] Christians, because these Christians are talking where they should be listening... One who cannot listen long and patiently will presently be talking beside the point and be never really speaking to others."

My wife told me of a painful college experience that illustrates this vividly. Her classmates had told her about a freshman adviser who was well liked, so my wife was pleased when she was assigned to her. Taking her class schedule in to be signed, she freely told the woman about some of her struggles adjusting to college life. In the middle of my wife's heartfelt sharing, the adviser interrupted—to correct her grammar. She made it clear, without so many words, that she wasn't interested in hearing what her young charge had to say. My wife never felt free to speak so openly with her again.

Little things can tell us if someone will be a good listener—for example, eyes that stay fixed upon us as we talk, as though nothing could distract their attention. A friend once described a good listener by mentioning the man's posture: "He *leans forward*—toward me—when I talk; it feels like he's willing to be intensely involved." By investing energy in listening, a mentor will help us feel important and valued.

Listening is important for another reason. Someone who takes time to listen is much more likely to offer counsel or encouragement that truly fits. A good listener will understand accurately our need or situation. My friend Jim, for example, *heard* something while we talked at the conference that helped him know that certain books would help me.

While words such as *direction* and *mentoring* imply taking charge and pointing the way, it is important to remember that a transforming friendship will allow us the space and quiet to be ourselves and to talk about what is happening deep within. Eugene Peterson has written that one characteristic of good spiritual

direction is to "get out of the way, to be unimportant...
A paradox is in operation here: to be *really* present
without being *obtrusively* present."

I know a woman who discovered this. The companion who taught her more about the spiritual life
than any other was careful not to give quick advice.
"We'd go out on a bike ride," my friend told me, "and
she'd let me talk while she just listened. She generally
didn't give an opinion, at least not right off. She'd ask
me probing questions that would bring me to my next
step."

The Encouragement of a Caring Friend

Just as important as being listened to—perhaps even
more so—is feeling acceptance. Some of the most
powerful changes within us will be spurred on by
affirmation, not criticism; encouragement, not neg-
ativity.

A former student of short-story writer Raymond
Carver recalled his teacher's belief in encouragement:
"One day, when I berated for going easy on a student I
thought was turning out poor work, he told me a story:
he had recently been a judge in a prestigious fiction
contest. The unanimous winner, whose work has since
drawn much praise, turned out to be a former student
of his, probably the worst, least promising student he'd
had in twenty years. 'What if I had discouraged him?'
he said."

Centuries ago Basil wrote that the spiritual guide
"must care for weak souls with tenderness and
humility of heart... He must be compassionate and

long suffering with those who through inexperience fall short in duty. He should not pass over their sins in silence, but must bear gently with the sinner, applying remedies in all kindness and moderation." It was with that sentiment in mind that spiritual writer Richard Foster once described a good spiritual companion as one who is "unjudging and unshakable."

I once led a feedback and support group for a pastor whose church had recently erupted in conflict. In one meeting the minister's wife told us, "Sometimes I need to share my frustrations with this group without feeling like you will try to talk me out of what I'm feeling. Sometimes I just want to express my tangled feelings and know I will be heard, know I am still okay." Our acceptance mattered far more than any answers we might give.

The Toughness of an Honest Friend

Sometimes, particularly when we feel ourselves in a rut or are too close to a situation to see it clearly, correction can be invaluable. We all need at least one person who will help us stay honest with others and ourselves.

James Houston writes, "Sin always tends to make us blind to our own faults... We need a friend to stop us from deceiving ourselves that what we are doing is not so bad after all. We need a friend to help us overcome our low self-image, inflated self-importance, selfishness, pride, our deceitful nature, our dangerous fantasies, and so much else."

In the eleventh century, King Henry III of Bavaria

grew tired of court life and the pressures of being king. He applied to a nearby monastery to join their order and spend the rest of his life in prayer with them.

"Your majesty," said Prior Richard, "do you understand that the pledge here is one of obedience? That will be hard because you have been a king."

"I understand," said Henry. "The rest of my life I will be obedient to you, as Christ leads."

"Then I will tell you what to do," said Prior Richard. "Go back to your throne and serve faithfully in the place where God has put you."

A relationship of accountability can help us stay true to our calling and resist the temptation to be less than we should be. "A mentor," a friend of mine likes to say, "is a friend who is tough enough to bring out the best in his student."

My friend Bill discovered this while in college. "There were the normal pressures of school, and spiritually I felt like I was not making it as a Christian," he said. "One night I trudged over to my friend Mike's apartment. 'I can't do it. I just can't live the Christian life,' I told him. He looked at me and said, 'I'm glad you finally realized that.'

"That comment didn't strike me as particularly compassionate at the time, but it was exactly what I needed. It was like a bracing slap on the cheeks. He went on to explain how I *couldn't* live the Christian life on my own power. What he said that night awakened me to a whole new dimension: I realized that if I were to be a Christian it would be through God living through me, helping me."

The Wisdom of a Spirit-Minded Friend

Careful listening and gritty honesty are vital, but the primary quality needed in a helper is spiritual wisdom. The center of spiritual direction has to do with our relationship with God, with becoming more like the Christ whom we try to follow. In a spiritual friendship, each person should see himself or herself as a seeker, involved in a process in which divine wisdom, not human expertise, is the ultimate standard.

Writing in the New Testament, Paul the apostle captured the significance of this. "We do not preach ourselves," he wrote, "but Jesus Christ as Lord, and ourselves as your servants for Christ's sake." Paul prayed for one church under his charge, "I keep asking that the *God of our Lord Jesus Christ*, the glorious Father, may give you the Spirit of wisdom and revelation, so that you may know him better." The focus of spiritual friendship, then, should never be on personality or human ingenuity, but on God and his work in our lives.

One woman I know had an extremely helpful relationship with an older woman who was very much a spiritual mentor. But, my friend told me, "she did not get me 'hooked' on her in a dependent relationship. I felt from her a deep respect and the belief that I can hear for myself what God might be saying or how he might be leading. She encouraged me time and time again to listen to what *I* was hearing and be confident of that voice." Her spiritual life grew immeasurably from the presence of this spiritually gifted friend.

Before we discuss actually seeking (and finding) a person with such traits, we need to see the different forms that spiritual companionship can take. To that we will turn in the next chapter.

For Further Reflection

☞ Name five people who have had the greatest positive impact on your life. For example, your list may contain the names of a parent, coworker or minister. Try to include people from both childhood and adulthood. Then, list the traits or qualities that made these people so important to your growth.

☞ How important to you are the four traits of an "unshakable companion" enumerated in this chapter? Is finding someone who will be kind and affirming more important to you than finding someone who can be tough? Do you agree that spiritual wisdom and maturity are among the most important qualities of a spiritual guide?

☞ Write a paragraph or two describing the qualities you would look for in an ideal spiritual helper. Make a list of the people you know that best demonstrate the traits mentioned in this chapter and in your paragraph(s). Can you envision any of them being your spiritual helper? Can you see yourself asking that person for help?

CHAPTER FOUR

Honey from More Than One Flower

Just as there is no universal remedy which is prescribed for every disease, so also there is no general guidance so perfect that every person, with his particular needs, can be helped by it.

Francis Quilloré, seventeenth-century French Christian

There is no problem, it seems to me, in collecting from many different flowers the honey which we cannot find in one flower only.

Francis of Sales

Friends are an aid to the young, to guard them from error; to the elderly, to attend to their wants and to supplement their failing power of action; to those in the prime of life, to assist them to noble deeds.

Aristotle

47

In the past few years, job changes have taken my family and me to several entirely new suburbs and small towns. Shortly after our last move, I began to feel that something was lacking. I had found acquaintances in my workplace and had met a few of our neighbors, but I missed having a companion in whom I could confide spiritual matters. Having read about spiritual directors, I assumed that was just what I needed. But who?

I asked a coworker whom I thought would know about such things. He gave me the name of a nearby retreat center, which had several spiritual directors in residence. I made contact, and was assigned someone. With some trepidation, I called and talked with a warm, sensible-sounding woman. We scheduled an appointment, and I began meeting with Marjorie every six weeks or so.

I still remember the rested feeling I had walking from the parking lot into the center's atmosphere of calm and devotion. More than once I thought, *What a luxury!* To be able to spend an hour with another person with no other agenda but to discuss my spiritual discoveries and longings for growth—this seemed like a rich gift.

But something else also began to take place. I had started meeting with my friend Bill, and our weekly meetings became an increasing source of support and insight for me. While Bill had little background in spiritual guidance, I found that our goals for prayer were similar, and his observations hit the mark in a way I had never experienced. After consulting with others, I decided that this was the relationship that deserved my concentration. I thanked my "official" spiritual director for her help and brought our relationship to a cordial close.

Help from the Unexpected Place

The last thing a person should do when thinking about spiritual companionship is assume that there is only one way to find it. Some of the best candidates around us may not be professionally trained. They may be of different ages. They may be our peers or more advanced than we are in things spiritual. And we may find that looking to one person for all our spiritual needs may not be realistic. We need to be flexible and creative.

We especially need to leave behind the assumption that those with a showy religious vocabulary are the only ones who can help. A person can use spiritual-sounding jargon in a convincing way, without possessing the maturity or depth to match. We sometimes need to look beyond the most obvious choices to find someone who truly can help us.

Eugene Peterson tells of finding his greatest help in an unlikely place. He had just come home for the summer after his second year in college, full of "unfocused energies and subterranean feelings that were looking for an outlet and not finding one... I thought the feelings had to do with God, but I wasn't sure. They were not fitting into the categories of faith I was familiar with."

An earlier attempt at finding a helper (in the person of his church's minister) had left Peterson stranded.

"After listening to me for about five minutes, he diagnosed my problem as sex, and launched into a rambling exposition on the subject." A second visit shed no more light on what he was experiencing, and Peterson concluded that he had gone to the wrong person. In the end, the most beneficial spiritual advice came from Reuben Lance, a gruff village character with a wild red beard, a jack-of-all-trades who was an "expert in everything manual: carpentry, plumbing, electrical work, masonry." Through unassuming, prayerful conversation, Reuben brought Peterson to a new understanding of God and his work in his life.

On Not Missing the Obvious

The first place to look for a spiritual friend is among the people we rub shoulders with daily—those who work in our offices, cut our hair, share with us in civic responsibilities or serve with us on church committees. These friends may have an experience to relate, a conviction to share or encouragement to give.

If we are alert, we may glean revelations from daily conversations. Talks with my wife while we take a stroll around the block have touched off new insights in me more times than I can count. Or sometimes a public speaker shares an experience or struggle similar to my own; something clicks, and I realize anew how much I can learn just by listening.

My friend Kathy went biking or walking almost every day with her neighbor. They did far more than discuss their children's school achievements or the latest novel they had read; they shared spiritual struggles. Their relationship grew to the point that they could pray for one another's doubts, joys and future growth.

Where Two or Three Are Gathered

We can also be creative about the number of people we involve in our spiritual growth. While most of this book assumes a one-on-one relationship, sometimes groups are helpful. When two people are inexperienced in giving spiritual guidance, for instance, the safeguards of a group's collective wisdom are valuable.

Group-centered spiritual direction took form in eighteenth-century England, when John Wesley, the founder of Methodism, struggled to help new converts grow in their spiritual maturity. The solution came in a surprising way.

The Methodists had contracted a debt to build a "preaching house." In an effort to pay off the debt, the leaders volunteered to visit each member weekly to collect a penny. But they soon found that it was easier for the people to come to the leaders. As people gathered for these "class meetings," the focus changed. Class leaders began to use the time to keep track of members' spiritual lives. Members opened up and talked about their progress and setbacks in living the Christian life; the groups discussed the issues raised; and the meetings closed with specific prayer for each person there.

Today house churches, Bible studies and special-interest groups allow the same personal sharing, feedback and prayer for members' needs. While these groups may not allow the focus on individual growth that spiritual companionship does, they make a good alternative.

I discovered this a couple of years ago. I began meeting with two other men from my church for an hour and a half every other Saturday morning. As we met, we talked about what God wanted us to be as spouses, fathers, church members and employees. We shared questions about our progress in faithfulness and Scripture verses that had helped us in the time since our last meeting. One of us read a passage from the Bible, and then we went around the circle and talked about our lives. We ended with informal, spontaneous prayer for one another.

"It had been quite a while since I could share deeply with other men," Steve, a member of the group, told me. "But it meant so much to have a close enough relationship to let down the masks and be known at a deep level."

A group approach worked well for another friend. She joined three other women who agreed to meet together regularly for one year, for the express purpose of working on spiritual growth. Each was to write in her journal regularly, read Scripture, pray, read an assigned book on some aspect of the spiritual life, and bring to each of the meetings the discoveries and struggles of the week.

Rose Mary Dougherty, director for spiritual guidance at the Shalem Institute for Spiritual Formation, Washington, D.C., leads many such spiritual-growth groups. "In group spiritual direction," she writes, "participants often hear God's word for them through dialogue. This is true even though the focus is on a single person at any given time... Sharing by members of the groups offers collective wisdom for each person."

The Options of Age

Spiritual guidance can come from people older than we are, younger than we are or the same age. Take, for example, an age-level peer. He or she may be asking the same questions we are, and thus be uniquely able to understand our struggles. That may mean more to us than sage, seasoned advice. Or an older partner's maturity and experience may be most appealing, particularly if we want tested wisdom and concrete suggestions for improving our relationship with God. However we choose, it is important to remember that age—and age differences—color the dynamics of any relationship.

Psychologist Daniel Levinson has found that we tend to see other persons as our peers if they are not more than six or seven years older or younger. When ages differ eight to fifteen years in either direction, we quite naturally regard the older one as we would an older brother or sister. A man of forty is regarded by people in their twenties as "Dad" rather than a buddy. In an age difference of forty years, the elder will assume the symbolic properties of a grandparent.

Think about the kind of guidance that will be the most helpful. Remember that siblings, parents, grandparents and even children have the ability to offer perspective and help. If we find ourselves drawn to people in one category only, we may want to expand our horizons.

Help from Many Sources

Even if we opt for a one-on-one approach, we may find it helpful not to rely on just one such relationship; there is no need to limit ourselves to one guide. We may need several, as another friend of mine discovered. He told me of a time when he struggled with a constant, seemingly unconquerable compulsion. "I was sincere in wanting to quit, but I seemed unable to stop." In his frustration, he turned to two men who were to help him in two very different yet complementary ways.

Charles went first to his counseling instructor at college, who was also a hospital chaplain. "He had little advice," Charles told me, "but communicated what I can only call unconditional acceptance. I find it hard to say what he did for me in that encounter, except to say that he conveyed an acceptance I had never before experienced. It has kept me going ever since."

But Charles did not stop there. He went to a philosophy instructor too. "He led me to the great fourth-century church leader Augustine," Charles explained, a writer and thinker who talked about the priority of the will in belief and Christian living.

While this second friend was accepting and caring, he also urged Charles to believe that change was possible, that the certainty of the Christian faith brings power to resolve struggles and end undesirable actions.

Charles discovered that each man contributed something different but vital. Through one, he learned anew to accept himself and trust God's ability to love him, whatever his failings. Through the other, he was nudged and pushed to believe that he must and, just as important, *could* change.

The people who walk in and out of our lives can make that kind of difference. We need only think creatively of the possibilities awaiting our initiative.

For Further Reflection

☛ Recall an experience when you gained unexpected insight from an acquaintance. Do you agree that "if we are alert, we may glean revelations from daily conversations"?

☛ Make a list of acquaintances in whom you could confide your spiritual questions.

☛ Recall how small groups—whatever their focus or context—have helped you. Think, for example, about parent-support groups, class-study groups or lecture and discussion groups. What were the advantages of working in a small group? How might those advantages transfer to a small group with a spiritual focus?

☛ Think about peers who are friends. Do their ages confirm Levinson's assertion that peers are not more than six or seven years older or younger?

On a sheet of paper, list the advantages of peers and elders under their respective headings. Which category seems best suited to your needs?

☛ Think of a question that has to do with understanding or relating to God that you would be comfortable asking someone. Now ask your question of more than one person. Does your experience confirm Charles's, that different people can offer a different, but complementary, perspective? What implications does this have for finding one or more spiritual companions?

DEVELOPING
THE
RELATIONSHIP

CHAPTER FIVE

Taking the Plunge

I once [asked] the Swiss psychologist Paul Tournier, "How do you help your patients get rid of their fears?"

"I don't," he said. "Fear is wonderful. Everything that's worthwhile in life is scary. Choosing a school, choosing a career, getting married, having kids—all the good things are scary. Don't get rid of your fears; look for fear. Do the thing you're afraid to do."

Bruce Larson

Let your acquaintances be many, but let your advisers be one in a thousand.

Ecclesiasticus, in the Apocrypha

[When it comes to spiritual companions,] choose one person among a thousand, one says. But I say, among ten thousand, for there are fewer than can be imagined who are fitted for this ministry. He must be filled with compassion,

*knowledge, and prudence; if one of these three
qualities is lacking in him, there is danger.*

Francis of Sales

A friend of mine, learning of my interest in spiritual helpers, wistfully remarked, "I don't have someone in my life like that, but I wish I did." That this friendly, socially competent man had no special friend isn't terribly surprising. Pollster Daniel Yankelovich has found that seventy per cent of Americans say they have many acquaintances but few close friends and that they experience this as a void in their lives.

We cannot always translate our desires into reality. Sometimes circumstances thwart our good intentions. But a lack of spiritual companionship often has to do with not knowing the concrete steps to take to find it. What follows is a plan of action.

A Wisdom Not Mine Own

The first and perhaps most important step is simple. We pray. We seek divine guidance. If all the great writers on spiritual friendship and direction say anything in common, it is that true spiritual help is more than a human enterprise. Spiritual direction hinges on revealed truth and godly insight. It stands to reason, then, that finding a helper means carefully listening not only to our own feelings and needs, but to ways God might be leading us.

Ralph, a colleague, discovered this when he realized that not since before he was married had he had a close friend with whom he could share spiritual matters.

When he heard two men discussing the nurture and guidance they received from a spiritual director, he remembered what it had been like. He started praying. "I wondered if I could find that one person in fifty who could listen to my soul." He began to pray simply, "Lord, bring along that kind of person."

It took a couple of years before the answer came. Ralph's company hired a new employee, who Ralph immediately suspected had potential to be a spiritual friend. Discussions in the hallway confirmed Ralph's hunch, but he continued praying for guidance. In the midst of his waiting prayer, Ralph's new friend came to *him* and asked about meeting together regularly for prayer and support.

Praying, of course, does not guarantee that we will always make perfect choices. It can, however, keep us open to God's sometimes surprising possibilities. Personally, spending time with God lets me more clearly discern the traits that should be present in a spiritual companion. When I pray, therefore, I try not only to present requests, but also to *listen*.

At the root of our seeking is the conviction, held by believers for centuries, that God does indeed respond to our requests. He is capable of showing us more than we usually realize. God does guide—often subtly, to be sure, but reliably nonetheless. Sometimes he simply waits for our asking before he moves in response.

With Eyes Wide Open
While praying, we can begin looking. As we think about those who manifest the qualities we need in a

spiritual friend, we will probably ask, "Lord, is *this* person the one?"

We may find that this stage takes time. We should not feel hurried or harried. Better to stay alert, to wait prayerfully and proceed only when the time is right. The answer may come when we least expect it.

When Ben Johnson, a teacher, began to ask himself who could provide spiritual guidance, he found that he rejected the names on his list one by one. "Some were too [emotionally] close; others were colleagues on the same faculty, or persons about whom I felt doubt. One person...was too busy; another, too far away. I considered the retreat master of the Monastery of the Holy Spirit. I also thought about going to a Jesuit priest. None of the options seemed right for me." So Ben was patient.

One day a friend mentioned a man known to be wise in spiritual matters, and he declared, "I'd drive halfway across the country to spend a day with John." Ben suddenly thought to himself, *That's it! He's the man!* He made an appointment, and he and his newfound helper decided that they would meet together as spiritual friends.

More Ways to Look

As we look, we should not overlook the obvious. A trusted pastor or teacher might be more than willing to become a spiritual helper, for example. Perhaps a grandparent, spouse or uncle could be enlisted.

One writer on the spiritual life has another suggestion. If your daily relationships fail to yield the helpers you need, he says, seek them out in exactly the same way you would seek a dentist when in a strange town: ask family and friends for recommendations.

Minding the Nuts and Bolts

Think about specifics. Count the cost. Plan realistically, deciding how your newfound companion will fit into the routines of your life. What kind of time can you give, for example? If the person you select is a two-hours' drive away, think how the distance will affect the frequency of your meetings.

Also think about the potential impact on those closest to you. Communicate clearly with a spouse or child or close friend what you are doing. Openness may keep a spouse from resenting the time this new relationship takes. Or it may keep jealousy from taking root if someone close to you feels excluded or threatened by this relationship.

One man I know decided to wait until he had been married several years before seeking out a spiritual companion. "My wife and I had a high-dependency relationship. We expected each other to be spouse, lover, confidant and counselor. It would have been too threatening to her. But after being married five, six years, she knew she couldn't meet all my needs, and that that was okay, that if I had a close friendship with another she wouldn't feel pushed aside or left out."

On Not Shrinking Back

Eventually, we need to settle on someone. We not only pray, think and discuss. We act. And perhaps this is hardest of all. It is one thing to become convinced that someone can guide us wisely. It is quite another to have the courage to risk asking.

Who knows? The person we ask may not understand, may think us odd. Or even worse, as one man who hesitated to approach a friend admitted, "I was afraid that I would be more interested in such a thing than my friend and that I would thereby place him in the awkward position of having to say no. I was worried that that would strain our existing friendship."

Beyond rejection, we also fear self-disclosure. Even if we feel reasonably sure that someone will be willing, we still may find ourselves hesitating. Procrastinating.

The reason is clear. Few things frighten us more than exposing our imperfect selves. It is vastly more comfortable, and unfortunately sometimes more rewarding, to be "on top." It is tempting sometimes, as a friend says, to share only the highlights, remaining quiet about the "lowlights"—those things that we would rather hide and keep to ourselves. Everyone ends up thinking that others are farther along. A mentality of rugged individualism tells us that it is weakness to seek another's help, that we are failures if we admit we are in need. The message is that if a person has problems, he should just try harder—on his own.

But the testimony of countless people is that the embarrassing, sometimes painful act of baring our souls to another produces much growth. With so much to be gained, it is easy to see that it is the voice of pride, not reason, that would isolate us and keep our questions and need for friendship to ourselves.

But the issue may be deeper. If hurt lingers within us from a previous disappointment or betrayal, exposing ourselves again could be an intimidating prospect. We fear that another will ridicule us, or shrug off our feelings as childish or insignificant. Such an emotional block is usually not painlessly overcome.

The loneliness and painful isolation of *not* seeking a friend, however, may propel us to the point of holy desperation. It may bring us to the place where we are willing to risk looking foolish or unsophisticated or imperfect.

Two Steps Forward, One Step Back

Finally, we need to remember that trial and error is sometimes the best way to reach a goal, especially when we are daring something new. Some corporations will not hire top-level management prospects *unless* they have at least one failure on their professional résumés. Those who do not, they reason, have never risked enough to fail, have never had the wholesomely painful experience of learning from a mistake.

Truth is, we often learn more about ourselves when we try something that does not work. When I brought my relationship with Marjorie, my first spiritual director, to a close, I felt that more important than the insights I absorbed from her were the things I learned about myself and my spiritual goals. I now knew the qualities I needed in a companion.

If you're not sure what you're looking for in a spiritual helper, begin the process of seeking anyway.

Your steps, even if faltering, will start you on the journey. If you don't find what you hoped for in the first person, think about what was lacking and look for it in the next person.

The risks of opening our lives to another are well worth it. And once we take this first step, the wonder—and the work—has only just begun.

For Further Reflection

☞ Begin praying, if you have not already, for God to provide the right person to help you in your spiritual journey. Simply say, "Lord, lead me to the person who can help me grow in my relationship with you. Give me patience while I wait for you to show me your will."

☞ Pray specifically about names that may come to mind in the next several days. If no names present themselves, consider the possibility that God has someone in mind but the timing is not right. You might also turn to friends or clergy for advice on who can help. Combine your prayerful weighing with hardheaded thinking about how each potential helper might work. Narrow down the possibilities.

☞ Find out what you can about the people you are considering from people who know them.

☞ By talking it over with a spouse or loved one, think

clearly about the time involved in meeting regularly with a spiritual helper. How often will you meet? How far will you travel to get together? What other practical considerations need attention?

☛ Unless you have strong reservations, or have found no satisfactory name, take the plunge! Take the initiative and invite your prospect to be your helper and friend.

CHAPTER SIX

Getting the Most Out of Spiritual Guidance

The best mirror is an old friend.

George Herbert

We do not wish for friends to feed and clothe our bodies...but to do the like office to our spirits.

Henry David Thoreau

To let friendship die away by negligence and silence is certainly not wise. It is voluntarily to throw away one of the greatest comforts of this weary pilgrimage.

Samuel Johnson

My seven-year-old son loves to dawdle. Even when the family is late for an appointment, Micah has an annoying habit of noticing things along the way—an odd-shaped piece of glass, a bottle cap on the pavement, a furry caterpillar inching across the front lawn. These "finds" so captivate him that he's always the last one in the car.

I cannot get too angry. More than his preoccupied father, Micah has a capacity to live intensely in the present, to observe his world with lively concentration. While he has some things to learn about promptness, he has much to teach me about alertness.

I sometimes let important experiences roll by without really watching or learning from them. I'm sometimes in a big hurry for little reasons, or I simply don't pay attention. "We get through life somehow on automatic pilot," Frederick Buechner once said, "not really listening, not really seeing even those who are closest, nearest and dearest to us, just getting through our lives."

The same can be said of a relationship with a spiritual helper. We can just "get through" our times together, allowing our discussion to skim the surface. Though presented with a world of insight, we can miss its life-changing potential.

What can we do to draw deeply from the insights that come to us? What qualities should we cultivate for a productive relationship with a spiritual friend?

Unlearning and Leaving Behind

First, I need openness to another's perspective. This is not so difficult when I feel at the end of my rope, when I'm tired of struggling with a persistent problem. More often, I hesitate: My alibis and spiritual laziness may not stand a wise friend's scrutiny. I may have to face up to the shallowness of prayers that rarely go beyond "Help me, Lord." I may find I have grown up with skewed, even damaging, pictures of who God is and what he is like.

But, writes James Houston, "a spiritual friend is someone with whom it is safe to take apart our shallow faith, our compulsive addictions, or whatever else might be under the surface of our visible lives.... We have been born into and grown up in a culture which is deeply alienated from God. So as we cross the border into God's kingdom, with its radically new attitudes and priorities, we will need all the help we can get from a spiritual friend who has made the same perilous journey before."

Over the years, I have discovered within myself an inordinate need for others' approval. My longing for acceptance has not only brought extra pressures to daily relationships, it has also colored my image of God. A past mentor once pointed this out, gently reminding me that I was too hard on myself when it came to prayer, that I could not relax enough in God's presence to truly enjoy him.

As comforting and reassuring as that message could have sounded, I resisted it. I preferred instead to see myself as a radical Christian, a noble believer who practiced what others only preached. But when another friend suggested that I needed to rest more in God's promise of acceptance, to receive what God wanted to give as a gift, it became increasingly difficult for me to deny what my mentor was saying about my approach to prayer.

A spiritual helper also can shed new light on the content of our praying, helping us make prayer more than just asking for personal blessings. Our devotional life needs a wide range of praise to God, confession of sin, intercession for others, and thanksgiving for answers and blessings received. A wise friend can be a teacher who reminds us of the rich diversity of Christian praying, who stretches our thinking and practice, and who encourages us to try new forms of prayer.

Our mentors may even suggest a "rule" or outline of prayer for us to practice. This helps us not to get stuck on only one or two ways of cultivating the spiritual life. We may, for example, need rounding out in the areas of worship, Bible study and reflection, or prayerful concern for the needs of the world.

A friend may suggest that we begin keeping a spiritual journal. This recording of daily events, prayers and personal insights can be a tool for what has been called "the private fingering of ordinary experience." It also can provide concrete material for later discussions.

A guide's help need not be limited to what is said and taught. The practice of praying with a mentor for ten minutes at the end (or beginning) of a meeting may do more to mold and shape our own prayers, if we observe our friend's example, than spending an hour talking *about* prayer.

Three persons visited the early Egyptian hermit Anthony every year. Two of them would question him about their thoughts and their growth in sanctity and fellowship with God. The third, however, remained completely silent. After a long while, Anthony said to him, "You have been coming to me all this time, yet you never ask me anything." The other replied, "Father, it is enough for me just to *see* you."

Another's words—and example—can leave us changed if we stay open, eager and willing to grow.

Honesty and Holding Fast

If progress comes when I stay open to another's new insight, it also comes when I am honest about my questions or objections. Few things muddle a relationship more than unspoken reservations and secret disagreements. When my spiritual guide makes a comment that challenges me, I am tempted to smile in outward agreement, while inwardly protecting and justifying what I think or do. The honest interchange that could lead to fresh insight never takes place.

We must find the courage to speak what we really are feeling. Otherwise, we say what we *imagine* we should feel or desire. "This," wrote Thomas Merton, "for all our good intentions, is plain hypocrisy." The result is a web of conversation "spun out of jargon and pious phrases which we have lifted from books and sermons and with which we conceal, rather than reveal, what is in us."

We need, then, to disagree openly sometimes. Only then can spiritual direction address our true selves. With our objections out on the table, they can be examined for what they are. (We may find that our guide has misunderstood something we have said.) Our honest reaction will ensure that the full picture is seen and that our mentor's suggestions hit the mark.

I have long struggled to be more frequent and constant in my times of prayer. I once was finding it particularly difficult to wake up early enough every morning to have a consistent prayer time before work. My spiritual mentor encouraged me not to worry. She encouraged me to find "pools of prime time" throughout the week—a half-hour here, two hours there—when I could withdraw and pray. As I experimented, though, I discovered that I am a morning person who does best getting an early start on things—including prayer. So I argued a bit. "I need to start my day with prayer," I told her. Out of our honest interchange, I came to appreciate both her encouragement to relax and my unique spiritual needs.

It is important to note, however, that honesty requires an atmosphere of trust. This will take time to develop. We do not share our darkest secrets, our most tenacious doubts, our gut reactions, with everyone. But deepening honesty should characterize any relationship that we look to for significant help. That means taking the risk of self-disclosure, pulling down the masks we use to hide our hurts and needs, and making ourselves vulnerable to the counsel of another.

Attentive to the Unseen Helper

Perhaps nothing is more important to the success of spiritual friendship than prayer. The underlying source of any growth is not ourselves or our helpers, but God himself.

I once saw a poster that showed two people looking heavenward, with the caption, "Love is not two people looking at each other, but two people looking in the same direction." The same can be said about spiritual direction. The focus is always ultimately beyond the two involved. In spiritual friendship, it is not enough that each friend listens to the other; both must listen to God. Listening is a waiting together on God.

We need to pray for our own growth and for our helper's continued insight. This should not be an onerous task. The Holy Spirit, who is both a helper and guide, can be trusted to prompt us. Says one man involved in a spiritual friendship, "It is amazing how often the Lord will bring my partner to mind. I believe it's the Holy Spirit's way of honoring our commitment to pray for one another."

This presence of an unseen helper is beautifully illustrated by the story of the English writer Evelyn Underhill's relationship to Baron von Hugel, the Catholic scholar who became her mentor. "Until about five years ago I had never had *any* personal experience of our Lord. I didn't know what it meant... But when I went to the Baron, somehow by his prayers or something, he compelled me to experience Christ... It took about four months—it was like watching the sun rise very slowly—and then suddenly one knew what it was... The New Testament, which once I couldn't make much of, or meditate on,...gets more and more alive and compellingly beautiful."

When the Going Gets Tough
Determination is another key to making the rela-tionship work. We discussed earlier the value of a

trial time for a new friendship, after which the partners feel free to evaluate and, possibly, end this aspect of their relationship. But even a trial time does not guarantee that tough issues will not surface later in the relationship. Any intimate relationship inevitably involves tense moments. Exposing one's deepest thoughts and longings opens up many opportunities for misunderstanding.

During difficult times, my temptation has always been to give up, go away and find another friend or helper. As we will see in the next chapter, there is an appropriate time for such change. But often growth comes only at those uncomfortable junctures when we successfully resist the urge to flee from a difficult situation.

In certain monastic orders, the brothers take what is known as a vow of stability. This is a commitment on their part to stay in their particular community even when it would be tempting to find another monastery.

A vow of stability makes sense for our friendships as well. Writer Thomas Merton comments that the insights into ourselves that our mentor provides may sometimes trouble us and be hard to accept. He warns: "At such a time we must be on our guard... We may be refusing to accept a grace which will transform our whole lives. We may be hesitating and turning back on the threshold of one of those 'conversions' which lead to a whole new level of spirituality and to deeper intimacy with Christ."

We need, then, to be careful not to react defensively to a hard word. When we find ourselves angry with our director, we need to sit up and take notice. Perhaps he or she has been unfair. But we may do well at least to try to go along with him or her for a time and see what comes of it. In no way, however, should we assume that disagreement or tension automatically means that something is wrong with our relationship.

As we commit ourselves to a transforming friendship, and as we pray expectantly and openly, we can expect God to use the insights—even the disagreements—to help us become the people God wants us to become.

For Further Reflection

☛ Think of a time when a new discovery forced you to revise your opinion of someone. Or recall a moment when you learned that a long-held prejudice was baseless. Why does it often seem frightening to change? How might such fear affect our openness to the new perspective of a spiritual helper?

☛ Do you agree with James Houston's statement that "we have been born into and grown up in a culture which is deeply alienated from God. So as we cross the border into God's kingdom, with its radically new attitudes and priorities, we will need all the help we can get from a spiritual friend"? Does his statement imply that growth often comes at the expense of old patterns of thinking?

☛ Recall a time when a friend or loved one confronted you with a hard truth about yourself. How did you react? What would you do differently now?

☛ Begin praying for your own spiritual growth. If you have a helper or friend, begin praying daily for him or her and for a growing, deepening relationship. Your prayers need not be elaborate, just heartfelt.

☛ Make a list of the things you can do to get more out of your relationship with your spiritual helper.

When It's Time to Move On

If a man does not make new acquaintances as he advances through life, he will soon find himself left alone. A man, sir, should keep his friendship in constant repair.

Samuel Johnson

When a soul has been under the direction of a spiritual father, and when it comes to meet some other, better one, it should resolve to leave the first... The soul that has this insight must, without concern for others' opinions, go freely where it finds its best director, going where God inspires it to go, and giving the new encounter every benefit.

Jean-Joseph Surrin, seventeenth-century French Christian

Be slow in choosing a friend, slower in changing.

Benjamin Franklin

A friend of mine once told me of his failed attempt at working with a spiritual helper and friend. "We realized shortly after starting out that things were not going to click. Week after week I would ask him, 'How's it going?' His answer was always, 'Fine.' But I knew from others who were close to him that things were not always fine. I would share some of my struggles, and we would pray together, but he couldn't seem to bring himself to share those places in his life that needed help."

When their trial period of six weeks was over, the two men agreed to stop meeting weekly. "It was hard to say, 'This isn't working.'" my friend recalls. "It was awkward, but there comes a time when you have to say, 'It's time to quit.'"

Despite our best efforts, we may choose a spiritual companion or helper whose theology or temperament or experience makes them ill-suited to us. Or, as we mature, we may find that a companion who seemed tailor-made for us at one stage in life becomes less beneficial at another.

My friend Rebecca had a director who taught her a tremendous amount about keeping a journal, relating to friends and listening for God's guidance. When Rebecca found herself in a difficult romantic relationship, she instinctively turned to her mentor. Much to her surprise, Rebecca found her mentor's temperament in this area so different that she could not gain much support from her. Rebecca had to find another friend for a sounding board.

Sexual attraction is another problem area. Such feelings on the part of either partner, should they become strong, could not only block spiritual progress; they could lead to disaster. Prudence may require openly discussing such feelings and ending the relationship, if necessary.

In the case of Eugene Peterson, two people simply found that their expectations for the nature of spiritual friendship conflicted, creating a distracting amount of tension. He asked an older man to be his spiritual mentor. This man had been in a wheelchair for forty years, but had a holiness and serenity about him that attracted Peterson. The two arranged to meet, but the encounter was a serious disappointment: "He was only interested in acquiring an audience for his 'wisdom' and proceeded to lecture me interminably from Ephesians for the three or four meetings that I had with him. I had no idea the Bible could be so dull... He saw me as an abyss of ignorance that he had been divinely appointed to fill in."

Whatever the reason, sometimes there comes a time to move on. The French priest and scholar Yves Ernest Masson writes, "Although it is best usually to confide in only one director, there is no need to be so completely attached to him. One should be sufficiently indifferent to him in order to be able to do without him; to be free to consult another, or even to change him altogether if need be."

What should you do if you find yourself restless after times with your spiritual friend, wondering if you have wasted time or, worse, been given inadequate counsel? How can you make a decision based on prudence and wisdom?

Take Care

Make certain that you are not avoiding painful issues that your friend or director may be raising for your benefit. Growth is rarely easy; it almost always involves letting go of pet conceptions that may be limiting or even damaging. Sometimes the hardest words can produce in us the greatest change and transformation. And even if your helper is clumsy or heavy-handed, there may be a great gift to be had if you humbly listen.

It may be important to remember, too, that there is no such thing as a perfect mentor. Even the most enlightened and sensitive spiritual guide can fail to respond to the delicate nuances of our character and struggles. This is all the more likely if we have not been open and honest with our companion or have not given him or her sufficient time to get to know us.

In this case, quitting or finding another companion would only lead us to repeat our failed encounters, always avoiding and never resolving the issues that keep us from deep and transforming encounters with God. We should not be hasty or haphazard.

Seek Counsel

When I was thinking about bringing my relationship with my first director to a close, feedback from others was invaluable. Talking about my decision ensured that my motives were solid, that I wasn't trying just to evade significant issues important to my growth.

Through my conversation, I realized that my lack of enthusiasm for that relationship was the result of a difference in our understanding of God and prayer. I also found that the additional input of others allowed me to be more confident and self-assured about my decision when I did decide to stop meeting with this mentor.

Take Courage

It is difficult to end or break off a relationship that we entered with high expectations. Not only may we feel some grief, there is always the risk that the other person will react angrily and reject us. We may fear that we will seem ungrateful or that our ending a relationship suggests we think ourselves somehow better than the other. The risk is worth taking, however, if the relationship has stopped being helpful.

The likelihood of hurt can be mitigated by our approach. Simple honesty, combined with appreciation for what we've learned, can help a break be clean and uncluttered. We should guard, on the one hand, against subterfuge and making excuses (for example, "Thirty minutes is really too far for me to drive every month to get together with you"). Yet neither do we have to be bluntly unkind. Months (or years) later, we may see in clearer light the wisdom of a director whose care is not to our liking right now. Humility is always in order.

We likely will find that our mentor understands our need for a change. Centuries ago John of the Cross, a great Spanish spiritual director, wrote:

"Spiritual directors should give freedom to people and support them in their desire to seek growth. The director does not know the means by which God may wish to honor a soul, especially if that soul is no longer satisfied with the director's counsel. This dissatisfaction is indeed a clear sign that the director is not helping the soul... These directors should themselves advise people to change. To do otherwise comes from foolish pride and possessiveness or some other personal need."

Consider leaving the door open for getting together more informally and infrequently, even after the regular meetings stop. Especially in the case of a friendship, the characteristics that first attracted you can continue to be a part of your life, now in a less-defined way.

Take Hope

When a friendship does not work out, it is tempting to conclude that it cannot *ever* work out. Instead, we need to learn from our experiences and trust that we will enter the next arrangement with a spiritual companion wiser and all the more ready to learn, grow and give to another.

Just as prayer for God's help and guidance is important in seeking and finding a guide, it is equally important in ending a relationship. Francis of Sales, the seventeenth-century French bishop, once wrote to a person in his care:

"Pray to God with great zeal, to provide you with a person after the heart of God, and have no doubt; for even though God should have to send an angel from heaven...he will give you a guide who is good and faithful... I say once more to you, pray to God to give you such a person, and, when you have received him, praise his divine Majesty, remain steadfast and do not search for any other, but travel on simply, humbly, and trustfully, for you will have a most beneficial journey."

Sometimes growing tension in a relationship of spiritual helping springs from an individual's growing maturity in the spiritual life. You may find yourself ready to impart insight to another, not just receive. If so, you may be ready for a helping relationship characterized by mutual growth, in which you and your partner guide each other. The chapters that follow will help in that movement.

For Further Reflection

☞ Think of an occasion when a friend or mentor's strong words prompted a new perspective. How did your reaction further or hinder your personal growth? Was the criticism fair? How did you know? What did you learn from the experience about coping with those who lovingly confront you?

☞ List the people you could talk to if you began to suspect your spiritual helper was not right for you. How might their varied perspectives keep you from a hasty or unwise decision?

☞ What issues could become a problem in your relationship with your spiritual mentor? Do any need action to ensure that areas of difference do not grow?

☞ Set up a time with your helper to evaluate the relationship. Be sure to affirm his or her strengths. Talk also about how the relationship can continue to be the best that it can be—for both of you. Plan to have regular times of evaluation and reassessment.

SHARING THE
BENEFITS

CHAPTER EIGHT

When Mentoring Becomes Mutual

The love of our neighbour is the only door out of the dungeon of self.

George MacDonald

What happiness, what confidence, what joy to have a person to whom you dare to speak on terms of equality as to another self. You need not be afraid to confess your failings to this person. You can also without shame make known whatever advances you have made in the spiritual life. You can entrust all the secrets of your heart to him and before him you can lay out all your plans... No bragging is to be feared and no suspicion need be feared. No correction of one by the other will cause pain, nor will praise on the part of one bring a charge of excessive flattery from the other.

Ailred of Rievaulx

When young Holden Caulfield of J.D. Salinger's *Catcher in the Rye* is moved by a crisis to visit a teacher he has loved, the old man assures him, "Many, many men have been just as troubled morally and spiritually as you are right now... You'll learn from them—if you want to. Just as some day, if you have something to offer, someone will learn something from you. It's a beautiful reciprocal arrangement."

Stan, a young friend, joined me in such a "reciprocal relationship" some years ago. A high-school senior, Stan was asking questions about his faith, which he had left behind for a time. He showed up at my church one Sunday and went out of his way to talk with me about his questions.

Then he attended a large regional youth conference that included speakers and workshop leaders, one of whom encouraged Stan to meet with someone regularly for Bible study. Stan returned from his meeting and asked if we could get together once a week. As we met, I found that Stan had the exuberant faith of a new convert.

His enthusiasm needed grounding in the wider perspective of Christian tradition, but his eagerness was contagious. Especially when it came to prayer. Not bothered by the finer points of theology, he simply wanted to experience as much of God's presence and power as he could. I found my own longing for a deeper experience of prayer challenged and encouraged by Stan's exuberance.

Driving alone in my car one February afternoon, shortly after we had begun meeting, I experienced a breakthrough in my praying. I uncovered an intensity in praise and communion not bound by words. The experience brought a depth and fluency in praying that has never been far from me since. My young friend, whom *I* was supposed to help (and did), was the catalyst for my own growth.

A Hand in Others' Growth

Christianity teaches not only that we can grow, but that we can in turn have a helping hand in others' growth. A child in the faith can mature and become someone else's spiritual father or sister. The one who learns becomes one who helps others learn, in a beautiful reciprocal relationship.

This is part of what Jesus had in mind when he used a startling image: "I am the vine, you are the branches," he told his disciples—his students. "If a man remains in me and I in him, he will bear much fruit... I no longer call you servants, because a servant does not know his master's business. Instead, I have called you friends, for everything that I learned from my Father *I have made known to you.*" Those who spent time with him, those in whom his life and influence had grown, would in turn have a fruitful effect on others.

This is also part of what the apostle Paul had in mind when he wrote to his younger charge, Timothy. While he calls Timothy his "true son in the faith," he also writes, "Don't let anyone look down on you because you are young, but set an example for the believers in speech, in life, in love, in faith and in purity."

This growth can take different forms. When our helper has many more years of maturity and experience, we may find the relationship always to be that of a learner and leader, mentor and protégé. But we may also find that a relationship that began with us as the student will evolve into a relationship of increasing equality and mutuality. You and your partner may become colleagues, able to support and help one another.

"The further the 'disciple' progresses," writes spiritual director Josef Sudbrack, "the more the 'master' must withdraw from the center of attention, must become not a 'master' but a 'companion' and even a 'disciple' himself."

In fact, we should beware of so revering a mentor or friend that we stop seeing their humanity and become unduly dependent. As one friend of mine wrote about her transforming relationship with another woman, "It would have been easy to exalt her at times because of how God used her in my life, but I've had enough experience in the last several years to respect the 'human' factor... There were times I saw her tired, stretched, hurried, or when the words and feedback didn't hit their mark. I think part of the nature of a mentoring relationship is to allow and respect that 'humanness' and to sift and sort when needed." Such awareness will provide for us the space we need for our own growth.

And even if the relationship with a spiritual helper does not change much as we mature, the outcome of a healthy mentoring or helping relationship will be our growing confidence in being able to hear the voice of God for ourselves. We may always want others to challenge or check or support us, but we should find ourselves more and more able to listen for ourselves, detecting God's work in our lives.

We should, in fact, never expect a mentor or companion to become a guru, or master, over all of our lives. "When a master promises satisfaction here and now," warns Josef Sudbrack, "when he offers something that Jesus treats as a gift of the Father, not to be realized until the coming of ultimate grace,...then he is not the one to show us the Christian way." Jesus got at this when he told his followers, "You are not to be called 'Rabbi,' for you have only one Master and you are all brothers."

Trying Your Wings

One way you may find an outlet for growing spiritual maturity is to begin to be a companion or guide for one who is also guiding you. Our focus in this chapter will be on the reciprocal relationship of *mutual* direction and helping.

When considering such a role, we need to remember that less important than years of training, certification in counseling or a degree in theology is our willingness to be used of God in listening, praying with and walking alongside the other. In the wake of the "professionalization" of our culture, where it is assumed that we can turn only to trained experts or specialists, our presence may mean all the more to someone. Our willingness to share ourselves— through encouragement and challenge—may bring us into an otherwise lonely life.

Others will not be the only ones to benefit. There is

something about sharing an insight that reinforces its impact and reality in our own lives. Ask teachers. One of the best ways to learn a subject is to *teach* it.

The Blind Leading the Blind?

In a relationship of mutual mentoring, some areas need special care.

First, there is the danger that your less-experienced companion in mutual mentoring may not have learned the importance of patient, painstaking listening. He or she may be too quick to offer advice. He or she may misread what we are saying and provide counsel not based on complete understanding. A friend may also suggest a wrong turn or be too tentative—less able, because of lack of confidence, to confront us when we are contemplating a misstep. Your mutual relationship may feel more like the "blind leading the blind." You may not feel the security you did from getting direction from an "old saint."

Second, if we come to experience a time of upheaval in our personal or spiritual lives, a mutual helping relationship may not provide the same time and attention that a relationship with a spiritual director might. Because our partner also looks to us for support, we may be afraid to dominate the time with our own needs—even when they are acute.

Finally, leadership will need to come somewhere, especially if the arrangement involves more than two persons. A formal leader is not necessary, but if an informal leader does not emerge, someone should be designated; informal groups often flounder if someone does not take initiative, ensure that meetings happen, and stay alert to the long-range goals and needs of those involved.

Sharing in the Depths

There are a number of advantages to mutual mentoring relationships.

We can usually learn and grow from hearing the struggles of another, for example. A friend once told me how he learned a lot about his own faith by watching his friend struggle through a time of tight finances. He told his friend, "The whole area of Christian giving was new to me. But I have heard you talk consistently about giving generously, even when you've not had anything to give. And when I know that I will see you regularly, it helps me when I face major purchases. I have to ask myself, 'Can I really go to a Christian brother and say this purchase is something God would approve of?' What I'm learning has nothing to do with anything you've said, just who you've *been*." We sharpen our perception of how God works by observing his action in the daily moments of another's life.

Mutual mentoring also gives us an opportunity for strengths to "rub off." I know of two men who began meeting together and discovered that each had a complementary perspective on the Christian faith. One was keen on character, asking questions such as, "Do you love your wife? Is your faith making a difference in the daily choices you make?" The other, while not discounting character, believed the core of the Christian life had to do with prayer, openness to the Spirit's leading, and how God's power can help us live abundant lives. Because they came together with respect, and yet had different insights, they helped each other move into greater wholeness and Christian maturity.

Finally, a relationship of mutual helping can keep us from becoming too inwardly focused, too caught up in every fleeting feeling of spiritual doubt, too absorbed by the workings of our own inward life. Spirituality should always strengthen us for the battle of faith, not let us retreat into an insulated, isolated inner world. Helping another reminds us that the goal of Christian growth is greater than our own warm feelings.

A medieval monk was responsible to open the monastery door each noon to distribute a daily ration of bread to the poor. One day, during an absorbing moment of prayer, Christ appeared to the monk in his cell. At the same moment, the noonday bell sounded. "What am I to do?" the man agonized. To leave Christ seemed irreverent. Yet to let the poor go hungry seemed cruel. He left, fulfilled his duty to his neighbors, and returned to his prayer cell, to find the Lord still there.

"I was afraid," he whispered, "that if I left, you would not be here when I returned."

"Did you think I would leave my poor ones?" came the reply. "Had you not gone to help and feed them, I would have had to leave to do so."

What we gain from our spiritual life, this story reminds us, is more than private fulfillment. Our growth should be shared with others. For some, that sharing will take place in a relationship of mutual mentoring. For others, it may take the form of being a director or mentor to another.

Whatever form it takes, drawing alongside another to help is full of both peril and great promise. The next two chapters offer guidance to help you avoid some detours and wrong turns, and brave the road ahead with more competence and confidence.

For Further Reflection

☛ What signs of growth might indicate to you that you are ready to do more than just receive insight—to pass it on to others?

☛ Do you agree with the statement in this chapter that "we should beware of so revering a mentor or friend that we stop seeing their humanness and become unduly dependent"? In your relationship with your spiritual helper, how great is this danger?

☛ What are some avenues already open for you to begin sharing the benefits of your spiritual maturity with others? Who do you know that might benefit, for example, from your gentle encouragement, or your being available to discuss spiritual issues? What obstacles might keep these encounters from taking place? What can you do to overcome them?

☛ Review the advantages and disadvantages of a mutual helping relationship. In your mind, what is the greatest advantage? Disadvantage? Do you feel ready to be a mutual mentor or special companion to someone? If not, what kind of maturity do you feel you need to cultivate to make that possible some day?

☛ If you already have begun to be a helper to someone, take five minutes now to pray for your partner. If you haven't, take five minutes to ask God if someone you know now needs your help, be it in a small way or large.

When Someone Seeks Your Help

A friend should bear his friend's infirmities.

William Shakespeare

One of the great rewards of loving God is being able to love others who also love him.

Saint-Evremond

Just as pure truth is seen only by the pure of heart, so also are a brother's miseries truly experienced only by one who has misery in his own heart. You will never have real mercy for the failings of another until you know and realize that you have the same failings in your soul.

Bernard of Clairvaux

Spiritual directors should soberly realize that they themselves are not the chief agent, guide, and mover of souls...but that the principal guide is the Holy Spirit.

John of the Cross

My friend Paul was brought up in an intensely religious environment. But for all the emphasis on the Bible, church and moral living, what praying he did was "slipshod, shallow and rarely more than an occasional 'God help me out of this jam!'"

Then Paul discovered the books of Helmut Thielicke, a German pastor and theologian famous for his ability to apply Jesus' teachings to modern people's desperate problems. Thielicke's sermons, prepared for people living through the devastation of Europe after World War II, made Paul aware of the emptiness of his praying. He began to pray about his *praying,* asking God to help him uncover a deeper relationship.

"The most amazing thing happened then," Paul recalls. Within a week after praying that new prayer, he found himself awakened in the early-morning hours—every morning at the same time. After several days, Paul recalls, "it dawned on me that maybe the Lord was answering my prayer. I got out of bed, went to my study, wrapped in a blanket, knelt at the couch, and said, 'Lord, I think this is your doing.'" It was the beginning of a decades-long habit of early-morning prayer. Paul's experience of God was immeasurably changed.

But Paul did not stop there. "Since then I have given away six cases of Thielicke books. And in the many groups of young people I've spoken to, when people say to me, 'I can't get my prayer life together,' time after time I've told the story of my discovery about prayer. I don't suggest they get up at the same hour I do, just that they go to the Lord like I did, and say, 'I really want to solve this problem. I'm inadequate here. Help me to find something that works.'" And they find it.

As we learn and grow from the influence of a spiritual helper, as Paul did, we can expect similar opportunities. The difference that begins to blossom within us will make others take notice and sometimes, perhaps, ask for help. What should we do?

When a Friend Comes Knocking

To begin with, remember that you may simply not be equipped for spiritual direction, however great your knowledge or experience. You may not have a natural facility in relating to others. Or you may simply not be drawn to the practice. There is no need to feel guilty if you feel more at home sharing yourself through writing, parenting, teaching, behind-the-scenes serving or helping the physically needy. The ways we help others are as varied as our personalities.

But what if we're not sure? How do we determine if we should become another's director or guiding friend?

First, pray. If the goal of spiritual direction is deepening a person's relationship with God—and if the wisdom for direction is rooted in prayer—the decision whether or not to direct another should grow out of prayerful reflection. As you pray, do your best to avoid assuming that you should or shouldn't direct another. As much as possible, entertain the possibility with an open mind. God sometimes surprises us with his leadings; he may have you do something for which you feel little ability (making his strength "perfect" in your weakness, to recall the memorable New Testament phrase).

On the other hand, you must be motivated by more than good feelings. The care of another's soul is too awesome a responsibility to undertake on a whim or out of an unstudied desire to be useful. God may tell you "Not yet." Or you may sense a definite "No" for reasons you do not understand at the time.

Joined with Others in Deciding

Enlist the counsel of your own spiritual helper or pastor. If you are part of a small group whose members are accustomed to praying for others' needs, think about asking the group to make your concern a matter of prayer.

Whatever you do, find someone who knows you well and can ensure that your decision to help another is wise. It is too easy to rush to help prematurely or for wrong reasons. Particularly when we are young in faith, still feeling the first flush of spiritual passion, we may not see all the complexities. A green, spring bud needs time to grow under the right conditions before it can produce fruit.

Watching Others Come

Take note of whether or not others come to you for advice about spiritual matters. If others suspect that you can be confided in, that you can shed light on their dark stretches and share in their joy, they will turn to you without your campaigning or advertising.

Avery Brooke, a publisher and writer, formed a group within her church to work on the church's newsletter. The group quickly took on the personality of a cadre of spiritual seekers—so much so that they were able to talk openly with one another about their struggles toward spiritual maturity. People in the church couldn't help noticing the growth that began to take place; surprisingly probing conversations about spiritual matters naturally blossomed between group members and the rest of the congregation.

"Suddenly we would find ourselves in a deeper and more personal place than we had expected. Haltingly, we would try to say something of the God we prayed to, of Christ, our companion in humanity and suffering whose life and death redeemed ours, and of the Spirit, that great inner Teacher."

How would you respond if friends or associates or relatives began to ask you about *your* discoveries and experiences? How would you feel if they turned to you for guidance? Aside from the anxiety and natural discomfort we all feel when trying something new and challenging, would you want to help? Or do you find yourself dreading the thought of such encounters? Your feelings are strong clues to whether or not you are ready to guide another.

A Confident Yes

If you have prayed, have sought another's counsel, have kept track of your feelings and now feel able to work at helping someone, do so humbly but confidently. Assuming responsibility for another's spiritual life is both more awesome and simpler than we might think.

I have a friend who has discovered this. "It has helped me to realize that an important part of what I do is to look simply for what God is already doing in this person's life. God has been working. My job is to help my friend see how God is already working and then see how current experiences fit into that work." Such an approach will be a relief to those mentors who feel that they have to know and notice everything.

It also means that effective spiritual direction will major on listening attentively to the other. Someone I know claims that 90 per cent of his effectiveness in relating to others has its roots in listening. As simple as it is, listening helps others relax. When we offer a listening ear, we offer a powerful reminder to others that God listens to them.

Our first question, then, is not, What am I going to say to this person? Or, How do I keep from saying the wrong thing? It is, How can I listen? What can I learn about this person—who they are, what they believe, what causes them struggle? Our primary role is not to provide answers, but to listen in a way that helps us, and our friend, listen for what God is saying.

We don't need a license in professional spiritual direction to help another. We mostly need to make ourselves available to others and convey in a simple way what we are learning about God. Do we have the patience and the desire to attend carefully to another's life? The answer to that question matters more than our degrees or years of experience.

In his book *The Wounded Healer,* Henri Nouwen retells a Jewish rabbinic legend that exemplifies the place of the spiritual mentor.

Rabbi Yoshua ben Levi once came upon Elijah the prophet while he was standing at the entrance to another rabbi's cave. He asked Elijah, "When will the Messiah come?" Elijah replied, "Go to the gates of the city and ask him yourself."

"How shall I know him?"

"He is sitting among the poor covered with wounds. The others unbind all their wounds at the same time and then bind them up again. But the Messiah unbinds one at a time and binds it up again, saying to himself, 'Perhaps I shall be needed: If so I must always be ready so as not to delay for a moment.'"

The Messiah, the story tells us, is waiting among the needy and poor for the time he will be needed. So it is with spiritual helpers. We are wounded healers; not perfect, not whole. Yet, through God's grace, we can still look after the wounds of others, even as we continue to be healed ourselves. What is most important is that we are ready to help if and when people ask.

We need not be overly anxious about the responsibility of assisting another in spiritual growth. But should we decide it is for us, there *are* things we need to learn, skills we can acquire, patterns we should emulate. In the final chapter, we will look at the skills we can (and must) acquire to be effective.

For Further Reflection

☛ Write down the most significant spiritual discovery you have made in recent months. Do you know someone who would benefit from its insight? Are there ways you can share it with your friend?

☛ Does the thought of talking with another about his or her spiritual life frighten you? How much of your fear can be chalked up to simple inexperience? How much do you think has to do with not being gifted in giving another counsel? Talk with your spiritual helper about your feelings and seek his or her feedback.

☛ Recall a time when someone sought your advice in an area for which you have special experience or expertise—from changing a flat tire to dealing with a rebellious child. What did you learn from the experience that might apply to sharing spiritual wisdom?

☛ Keep track of when people come to you for help in spiritual matters. Do you dread such encounters or look forward to them? What might your feelings tell you about whether or not you should take on someone as a spiritual partner or protégé?

☛ Begin regularly praying along these lines: "Lord, I want to be open to those around me who need to know about you. Open doors of opportunity for me to share, and guide my lips when I am called upon to speak about you." When a door opens, don't hesitate.

CHAPTER TEN

Directions for the Director

Love seeketh not itself to please,
Nor for itself hath any great care;
But for another gives its ease
And builds a heaven in hell's despair.

William Blake

Some directors get an idea and a plan into their heads, which they think much of, and apply to all the souls who come to them, thinking that they will accomplish something great if they bring them into line with it. They have no other object but carrying out what they have decided another should look like, as though they wish all should wear the same clothes.

Jean-Joseph Surrin

The [spiritual] instructor is not to teach his own way, nor any set way of prayer, but should instruct his disciples in how they may find a way

113

appropriate for them... In a word, he is only God's usher, and must lead souls in God's way and not his own.

Dom Augustine Baker, seventeenth-century monk

On his way home from work, George, a member of my church, often used to drive by my rural Virginia house on the road that curved around the front of our property. If I was in the yard, he sometimes would stop and talk. We would stand under the shade of two huge maples whose branches interlocked overhead, talking about his job with a road-construction crew, our young children or the intricate web of extended family relationships at the church we attended.

One time, as I leaned against one of the maple trunks, I shared with him—somewhat tentatively—some recent progress in my practice of prayer.

George responded with respect and wistfulness in his voice. For all his years of church attendance, he told me, he was bored and "frustrated" with his Christian life. "I feel like I have been studying Sunday school lessons for years, but never seem to get anywhere. In fact, lately I've gotten away from praying, and when I do pray, I have trouble knowing the words to say. I've taken to piling up big, theological-sounding words, so my prayers sound spiritual."

I cannot remember what I said in response, but I have never forgotten how I sensed immediately that I was witnessing a time of profound spiritual openness in a friend's life.

In our society, it seems, much nurturing is impromptu; spiritual direction takes place on the run. Riding together in the car, someone may start telling you about their interest in attending church. Or somebody pulls you aside after a meeting, passes you in the hall, approaches you in the parking lot. People often verbalize spiritual concerns, even if they mask them.

When someone says "Think about me" on their way into surgery, it usually means, "I need you to pray for me." When a friend confides anxiety about being able to pay the bills, there is usually an unspoken theological dimension (learning to trust). When a colleague confesses his temptation to get involved in an adulterous affair with a fellow employee, far more is at stake than office politics or his libido. If you are attentive, you can help. And it may set the stage for a deeper relationship.

One of the primary prerequisites for sharing, therefore, is alert sensitivity. Whether we help others in an official capacity as a spiritual director or not, we all need to be open to everyday opportunities to support or help another.

When You're Ready to Meet

Should you decide to make the helping relationship more structured, here are some suggestions on how it often works best.

Use an initial meeting or two to explore the relationship. If you are meeting with someone you do not know well, take time to get to know your charge or mutual helper. It is too easy to assume your charge is ignorant, when in fact there may be great experience or wisdom. Only as you know the person you are meeting with can you give help that hits the mark.

Ask questions. Why did he or she come to you? What are his or her spiritual goals? Are they in line with your understanding of the spiritual life? Be clear about seeing spiritual direction as helping someone grow in their relationship with God; it is not primarily counseling, teaching, confession or crisis intervention.

Be clear also that your interest as a helper will not primarily be one of friendship in the social sense (unless it is that already). When I served on a church pastoral staff some years ago, a young man in the congregation called me. He wanted, he said, to get together with me once or twice a week. "I need someone to go bowling with, to talk about my job, to be an 'official' friend." He asked this despite our rarely having talked before and our apparent lack of things in common. A part of him, I suspect, wanted spiritual guidance, but that somehow got mixed in with his request for friendship. Had he simply asked for spiritual help, I would have gladly said yes. But his expectations were fuzzy, and would have required a friendship commitment I was not prepared to give. I had to tell him gently no.

When It's Time to Draw the Line

Be alert to the possible need for drawing boundaries. Make certain your partner understands that spiritual helping is no substitute for in-depth counseling if your partner needs it—though it certainly can complement professional help.

My wife and I once gave spiritual direction to a woman I'll call Jeannine, who struggled with deep depression. Against everyone's advice (including ours), Jeannine dropped her regular sessions with her psychoanalyst. She began to look to us not only to give spiritual guidance, but to make up for the support her doctor had been giving her. She began asking for more than we had time or ability to give. We came to a painful point where we had to set clear limits.

Watch for times when you feel "in over your head" as a helper. If your partner is exhibiting aberrant, destructive or unexplainable behavior, if he or she is severely depressed, you may have a role to play in helping him or her to find professional help. Referring your friend to a pastor or counselor is a mark of compassion and wisdom, not abandonment.

On Not Breaking the "Rule"

Discuss a strategy for your partner's growth in prayer. Because the primary purpose of spiritual helping is to aid another's relationship with God, many directors find it helpful to agree upon a "rule" or discipline of prayer.

Formulation of a rule is not so difficult as it might seem. Most people seeking help for their spiritual life already have some practice established, even if it is a haphazard one. Chances are they pray at night before going to bed, say grace at meals, read the Bible or devotional books, or experience corporate prayer in church or at a weekly Bible study.

So begin where the person is. But also suggest things that need to be added, or help the person uncover and eliminate prayer practices which may not be fruitful.

The Shape of Help
As you meet with your friend, keep in mind these practical suggestions:

Provide clean, uncluttered physical surroundings. Your meeting place should not be a dingy cellar, a cluttered room, a noisy public place (such as a crowded restaurant), or an office where phone calls or unexpected company are likely to interrupt.

Begin with prayer. God's guidance is indispensable to the enterprise, and praying with your partner can provide valuable stability as you both begin.

Meet for a specified time. For a one-on-one arrangement, forty-five minutes to an hour should be enough. A relationship of mutual mentoring where both are sharing may take a bit more time.

Be alert to the feelings beneath the spoken words or outer expressions. Learn to read the soul of another, to listen with what has been called "love's third ear." Be ready to raise questions about the spiritual dimensions of what may initially seem mundane concerns.

Consider the role of church in your partner's life. If he or she avoids church participation or is on the fringe of institutional faith, consider ways to help the person initiate or re-establish a relationship with a church. Spiritual direction is no substitute for the regular nurture and challenge that comes from a group of believers. "Let us not give up meeting together" is the counsel of Scripture. Spiritual direction will be much more fruitful if your friend's needs for fellowship, worship and instruction are appropriately met in a congregation.

Be sensitive to ways you can help your friend cultivate the "fruit" of the Spirit. These include aspects of character such as love, joy, peace, patience, kindness and self-control. Explore together how these natural expressions of the Christian life can take practical form in daily life.

Consider ways you can suggest resources to the one you help. Books by writers such as Thomas à Kempis, Oswald Chambers, Thomas Kelly, Richard Foster and E.M. Bounds can be a wonderful complement to your instruction, strengthening a person's grasp of the spiritual life.

Keeping a journal may also be a productive practice for the one you help, especially as he or she explores aspects of vocation and direction for the future. The events, questions, prayers and insights recorded in a journal during the days between your meetings can be the basis for wonderfully enlightening discussions.

Something Never to Forget

Finally, it will be absolutely vital to remember that some of the most important parts of direction are unconscious. Who we *are* often matters more than what we say or do. That should be an encouragement both when we make mistakes (as everyone does) and when we actually help. Sometimes, in fact, it's the forgotten words or unselfconscious acts that matter greatly to others.

A spiritual helper is much like a midwife. A midwife can be a key player in delivery, especially when labor is difficult. A midwife must be well-trained, must stay alert, and often must work very hard. But just as the midwife is primarily a *helper,* so also with spiritual companions: We are called in to support and assist in the delivery of a new life, but we do not give the life itself. It comes from a Source above and beyond us. Sometimes we help most by not meddling, letting healing and growth and the birth of something new take its course.

As that kind of helping happens through us—and, through others, within us—we will be astounded by the joy of companionship. We will wonder how we ever did without such a relationship.

Whatever forms spiritual guidance takes in the years ahead, our lives will be incomparably richer for the help we gain and give.

For Further Reflection

☛ Do you agree that "in our society, much nurturing is impromptu," that spiritual direction often takes place on the run? Think of a time when your "alert sensitivity" allowed you to offer support or guidance to someone who was hurting. What were the signs that signaled your friend's need of help?

☛ When has someone asked too much of you, overstepping appropriate demands on your time and energy? How did you deal with their unrealistic expectations? What did you learn that might help you set limits as a spiritual helper now?

☛ What is your own "rule" for prayer and devotion? On a piece of paper, outline your typical prayer time. What are you doing that would help a friend seeking your advice?

☛ What does it mean that sometimes we help the most by not meddling and letting another's growth take its own course?

☛ Make a list of three spiritual practices that need developing in your own life, practices that will allow you to be a more spiritually sensitive and knowledgeable guide. Perhaps you need to read more books about ways to pray, or you need to be more regular at Bible study. For each of the three, take a separate sheet of paper and outline specific steps that will help you toward your goal. Commit your plans of action to God in prayer, and prepare to grow—for your sake, and that of others.

BIBLIOGRAPHY

BOOKS

Dietrich Bonhoeffer, *Life Together,* Harper & Row, 1954.

Avery Brooke, *Finding God in the World,* Harper & Row, 1989.

Frederick Buechner, *Now and Then,* Harper & Row, 1983.

Ben Campbell Johnson, *To Pray God's Will,* The Westminster Press, 1987.

Tilden Edwards, *Spiritual Friend,* Paulist Press, 1980.

Richard Foster, *Celebration of Discipline,* Harper & Row, 1978.

James Houston, *The Transforming Friendship,* Lion Publishing Corporation, 1989.

Alan Jones, *Spiritual Direction,* The Seabury Press, 1982.

Thomas à Kempis, *The Imitation of Christ,* I.

Thomas Mallon, *A Book of One's Own,* Ticknor & Fields, 1984.

Thomas Merton, *Spiritual Direction and Meditation,* The Liturgical Press, 1960.

Francis Kelly Nemeck and Marie Theresa Coombs, *The Way of Spiritual Direction,* Michael Glazier, 1985.

Jerome M. Neufelder and Mary C. Coelho, *Writings on Spiritual Direction by Great Christian Masters,* The Seabury Press, 1982.

J.D. Sallinger, *The Catcher in the Rye,* Little, Brown, 1945.

Josef Sudbrack, *Spiritual Guidance,* Paulist Press, 1983.

Charles R. Swindoll, *Encourage Me,* Multnomah Press, 1982.

ARTICLES

Rose Mary Dougherty, "Doing Spiritual Direction in a Group," *Praying,* March/April 1989.

Gary W. Downing, "Accountability That Makes Sense," *Leadership,* Spring 1988.

James M. Houston, "The Independence Myth," *Christianity Today,* 15 January 1990.

Jay McInerney, "Raymond Carver: A Still, Small Voice," *The New York Times Book Review,* 6 August 1989.

Eugene Peterson, "The Summer of My Discontent," *Christianity Today,* 15 January 1990.

REPORTS

Faith Development and Your Ministry, a report based on a Gallup survey conducted for the Religious Education Association of the United States and Canada by the Princeton Religious Research Center, Religious Education Association, 1985.